PRIMARY SOURCES IN AMERICAN HISTORY™

THE UNDERGROUND RAILROAD

A PRIMARY SOURCE HISTORY OF THE JOURNEY TO FREEDOM

PHILIP WOLNY

rosen central
Primary Source™

The Rosen Publishing Group, Inc., New York

To my parents, Julita and Mike Hetlof

Published in 2004 by The Rosen Publishing Group, Inc.
29 East 21st Street, New York, NY 10010

First Edition

Library of Congress Cataloging-in-Publication Data

Wolny, Philip.
The Underground Railroad: a primary source history of the journey to freedom/ Philip Wolny.— 1st ed.
    p. cm. — (Primary sources in American history)
Summary: Examines the events and key figures behind the formation and operation of the Underground Railroad, the secretive and illegal organization that helped American slaves escape to freedom in the northern United States and Canada.
Includes bibliographical references (p.) and index.
ISBN 0-8239-4008-X (library binding)
1. Underground railroad—Juvenile literature. 2. Antislavery movements—United States—History—19th century—Juvenile literature. 3. Antislavery movements—United States—History—19th century—Sources—Juvenile literature. 4. Fugitive slaves—United States—History—19th century—Juvenile literature. 5. Fugitive slaves—United States—History—19th century—Sources—Juvenile literature. [1. Underground railroad.
2. Antislavery movements. 3. Fugitive slaves.]
I. Title. II. Series.
E450.W85 2004
973.7'115—dc21

2002156011

Manufactured in the United States of America

On the front cover: A painting entitled The Underground Railroad by Charles T. Webber, c. 1893. Courtesy of the Cincinnati Art Museum.

On the back cover: first row (left to right): Immigrants arriving at Ellis Island; Generals Lee and Grant meet to discuss terms of Confederate surrender at Appomattox, Virginia. Second row (left to right): Lewis and Clark meeting with a western Indian tribe during the expedition of the Corps of Discovery; Napoleon at the signing of the Louisiana Purchase Treaty. Third row (left to right): Cherokees traveling along the Trail of Tears during their forced relocation west of the Mississippi River; escaped slaves traveling on the Underground Railroad.

CONTENTS

NTRODUCTION

Imagine you are hiding in a cramped closet. You can barely move your arms or legs. You try to remain as quiet as you can, but you can still hear the hushed voices of the four men and women crowded against you in the hot and suffocating space. You can almost taste the fear in the air around you.

Suddenly, you hear voices outside. A lot of movement seems to be occurring just on the other side of the wall. You hear shouts and rushing footsteps. Your heart almost skips a beat: You could be discovered at any moment!

THE LONG RIDE TO FREEDOM

But the voices suddenly fall silent, and you hear the sounds of horses riding away. You and your terrified companions wait for a while longer, your pulse pounding in your ears. Finally, the door to the closet flies open. You don't know what to expect as your eyes squint against the sudden lantern light in the room.

But the woman's face in the doorway is a familiar and friendly one. She tells you that the coast is clear and that those who are chasing you have moved on. One by one, all of you stiffly crawl out of your hiding place and stretch your cramped, road-weary limbs. Not a second can be wasted, however, as the woman leads you to the cellar. There, she moves a book on a bookshelf, and a false door swings open into a darkened passageway.

Once again on the run, you and your companions follow her down a rocky corridor. Finally, she pushes aside a pile of logs and brush, and you head out into the cool night air. After a quick run down an unfamiliar path, you are suddenly at the edge of a wide river. There, boats are waiting to take you up the coast of a great lake to Canada—and freedom.

The men and women described in this account were participating in one of history's noblest endeavors: the Underground Railroad. It was not a true railroad with trains, tracks, predictable schedules, and safe journeys. Instead, the Underground Railroad was a secret system of safe houses and courageous volunteers who helped fugitive slaves escape the South in the years before and during the U.S. Civil War. Many Underground Railroad agents risked life, limb, and property to help other men and women escape from bondage to seek the promise of freedom in the North.

The history of the Underground Railroad is distinguished by great creativity, courage, endurance, and faith. Its agents helped many thousands to live in freedom for the first time in their lives. The Underground Railroad's successes, and even its failures, helped to rally millions of other Americans against the institution of slavery. These are the true stories of some American heroes who, in their tireless efforts to help escaped slaves reach freedom, also helped abolish slavery in the United States.

TIMELINE

1775 — The Pennsylvania Abolition Society, the world's first abolitionist society, is founded by Anthony Benezet to protect runaway slaves and free blacks who were illegally captured and enslaved.

1777–1827 — All Northern states abolish slavery.

1793 — The Fugitive Slave Act becomes a federal law and allows slave owners and their agents to seize runaway slaves, even in free states and territories.

1804 — The Underground Railroad is unofficially inaugurated after slave owner General Thomas Boudes of Columbia, Pennsylvania, refuses to release escaped slaves to authorities.

1820 — The Missouri Compromise allows Missouri to enter the Union as a slave state, while Maine enters as a free state. It also outlaws slavery in any new states or territories north of the latitude 36°30'.

1838 — The Underground Railroad is formally organized.

TIMELINE

1849 — Harriet Tubman escapes slavery in Maryland. She will return to the South nineteen times to rescue several hundred slaves.

1850 — In exchange for agreeing to allow California to enter the Union as a free state, Southern congressmen pass a harsher Fugitive Slave Act.

1857 — The U.S. Supreme Court decides, in *Dred Scott v. Sandford*, that blacks can never be citizens, that Congress cannot outlaw slavery in any U.S. territory, and that slaveholders can recapture escaped slaves even in free areas of the country.

1860 — Republican candidate Abraham Lincoln is elected president of the United States.

1861 — The Civil War begins.

1863 — President Lincoln issues the Emancipation Proclamation, freeing all slaves throughout the nation, including the Confederate states.

1865 — The Civil War ends. The Thirteenth Amendment permanently abolishes slavery in the United States.

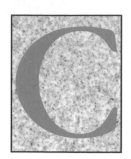

CHAPTER 1

Life, liberty, and the pursuit of happiness—these are considered to be the founding principles of the United States. These three ideals spurred the American colonies to fight for independence from England and to establish the first modern democracy. But for many people living in post–Revolutionary America, freedom was a dream that would remain unfulfilled for many years.

LAYING THE TRACKS

Slavery in America

Although the new nation was committed to equality and liberty, it denied the most basic freedoms to millions of its residents. Throughout the seventeenth, eighteenth, and first half of the nineteenth centuries, slavery was practiced in the United States. Africans were kidnapped from their homes and villages by slave traders; placed into crowded, disease-ridden ships and brought to America; and sold as slaves in public markets to landowners and merchants. This buying and selling of human beings was considered to be legal. In the pre–Civil War years, gaining a slave's freedom usually meant breaking the law. Freedom was something for which slaves would have to fight long and hard. Yet they would not fight alone. From free blacks to former slaves to Quakers and other white American abolitionists, the fight against slavery became a crusade to make America live up to its promises and ideals.

Illustrations of the American Anti-Slavery Almanac for 1840.

"Our Peculiar Domestic Institutions."

Northern Hospitality—New-York nine months law. [The Slave steps out of the Slave State, and his chains fall. A Free State, with another chain, stands ready to re-enslave him.]

Burning of McIntosh at St. Louis, in April, 1836.

Shewing how slavery improves the condition of the female sex.

The Negro Pew, or "Free" Seats for black Christians. | Mayor of New-York re-fusing a Carman's license to a colored Man.

Servility of the Northern States in arresting and returning fugitive Slaves.

Selling a Mother from her Child.

Hunting Slaves with dogs and guns. A Slave drowned by the dogs.

"Poor things, 'they can't take care of themselves.'"

Mothers with young Children at work in the field.

A Woman chained to a Girl, and a Man in irons at work in the field.

Branding Slaves.

Cutting up a Slave in Kentucky.

Paid.   Unpaid.

This broadside from 1840 is a collection of illustrations taken from the American Anti-Slavery Society's almanac of that year. The society published this work annually in an attempt to inform the public about the horrors of slavery. Each scene depicts the harsh world of the slave plantation, including images of forced labor, the splitting up of families at slave auctions, violent physical punishment, and hangings.

Millions of black Americans were in bondage, working as slaves on farms in the southern United States, raising many crops. One of the most important crops was cotton. Many proslavery forces believed that the South's power and wealth depended on the free labor that slaves provided. Many in the nation, particularly in the North, but a good number also in the South, opposed slavery. They thought that no human being should own another and take away his or her liberty and basic human dignity. Some slaves were often treated no better than animals and were whipped, beaten, and even killed for minor offenses.

The Abolitionist Movement

Though unpopular at first, an antislavery movement began to grow in strength and number. These antislavery activists were called abolitionists. To "abolish" means to "end or destroy something." Abolitionists wanted to outlaw slavery everywhere in the United States. Abolitionists had more early success in the North, where attitudes were more liberal and progressive, and the economy was not dependent upon slave labor. Between 1777 and 1827, all Northern states abolished slavery. Millions of slaves in the Southern states, however, remained captives.

Abolitionism slowly gained supporters. Many prominent religious and political leaders, as well as influential businessmen and society women, spoke against slavery at meetings in cities, towns, and villages throughout the North. Even though the Northern states had abolished slavery, it was still dangerous to speak one's mind on the subject. Abolitionists were sometimes lynched by angry mobs. Many in the North who had close business ties to agricultural production in the South thought of slavery as necessary to their economic well-being.

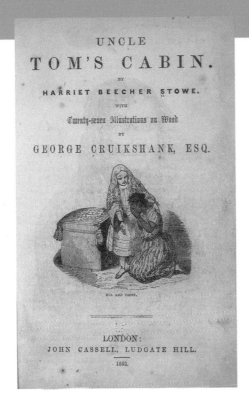

Perhaps one of the greatest events that won abolitionism widespread support was the publication of *Uncle Tom's Cabin*. Author Harriet Beecher Stowe, raised by die-hard abolitionists, based her tale of slave life on people she met while living in Cincinnati, Ohio, which bordered Kentucky, a slave state. On the left is the title page from a copy of the 1852 edition of the book published by John Cassell. On the right is a poster advertising the sale of Stowe's very popular and influential book.

Some abolitionists joined forces and started their own societies, or clubs, to help spread their message and further their cause. Many of these societies began their own newspapers dedicated to abolition, like William Lloyd Garrison's *Liberator*. They spoke in churches and halls throughout the country in an effort to end support of slavery through moral persuasion. Moderates, those who believed that change should be gradual, thought that changing people's minds was the first step to transforming society.

Pictured here is the Reynolds Political Map of the United States, which depicts the free and slave states circa the presidential election of 1856. In the upper left corner of the map is a portrait of John C. Fremont, the explorer-turned-presidential candidate for the newly formed Republican Party. In the upper right corner is his running mate, William L. Dayton. The Republican Party emerged out of the fight against the extension of slavery into the western frontiers of the United States.

Construction of the Underground Railroad

Other abolitionists, however, thought that change was not coming quickly enough. Believing that a more active approach was required, they decided to take matters into their own hands. Some traveled to the South and attempted to free slaves by helping them flee their masters. For these escapes to be successful, there needed to be a way of safely and secretly transporting escaped slaves to the North. Fugitive slaves were sometimes hidden in the homes of people who believed it was their moral duty to help their fellow human beings. Slowly, a loose network of "safe homes" developed, dedicated to helping fugitive slaves escape to freedom. The Underground Railroad was born.

At first, this escape system had no official name. Many of those helping the slaves escape worked in small, isolated groups and had little contact with other "stations" on the route. Plans to help fugitives were made by word of mouth. Rumors would spread, for example, that a certain person in a certain town would help. Hearing this, an abolitionist who lived a few towns away would send fugitives to that person. Sometimes a guide helped the escaped slaves travel between safe houses. Other times they had to fend for themselves.

As abolitionism grew, more and more people became involved in the Underground Railroad and began to communicate with each other. It became known that certain towns were abolitionist hot spots. Many of these were in Midwestern states such as Michigan, Ohio, Pennsylvania, Indiana, and Illinois. These states are near the Great Lakes, which border Canada, a destination for many escaped slaves. By the early nineteenth century, the various regions of that nation (which had not yet been divided into provinces) had ruled that slaves who left their masters were free and could not be forcibly returned to them. Meanwhile, other abolitionist groups interested in helping slaves escape to freedom began to form in New York, Philadelphia, and Boston. The tracks were being laid, so to speak, for a true network.

THE LIBERATOR.

VOL. I.]   WILLIAM LLOYD GARRISON AND ISAAC KNAPP, PUBLISHERS.   [NO. 1.

BOSTON, MASSACHUSETTS.]   OUR COUNTRY IS THE WORLD—OUR COUNTRYMEN ARE MANKIND.   [SATURDAY, JANUARY 1, 1831.

One of the most prominent abolitionists, William Lloyd Garrison *(inset)* published the *Liberator* every week from 1831 until the end of the Civil War and the passing of the Thirteenth Amendment to the Constitution, which abolished slavery, in 1865. Some Southern states banned the *Liberator* and made possession of it a crime. Garrison and his followers called for the immediate end to slavery in its pages week after week. This is a copy of the front page of the paper's first issue, dated January 1, 1831. See partial transcript on page 55.

William Lloyd Garrison and the Abolitionist Press

While some abolitionists threw their energy into the Underground Railroad, others were taking on the equally important and difficult task of convincing Americans that slavery was a great evil. They hoped to persuade Americans that it was slavery that should be made illegal, not helping enslaved human beings escape to freedom. They hoped to make the Underground Railroad—though a noble institution—obsolete by ending slavery and the illegal actions necessary to fight it.

The popular press provided the perfect platform for antislavery appeals to the public. In 1831, William Lloyd Garrison, a white newspaper editor, printed the first issue of his antislavery newspaper, the *Liberator*, which he published every week for the next thirty-four years. Garrison reached out to Boston's black community and to blacks nationwide, who were the majority of his first subscribers. At the time, Garrison's views were considered extreme, even though he sought change through nonviolent means and called for a voluntary, nationwide rejection of slavery (rather than forcing people to abandon slavery by outlawing it).

The efforts of the abolitionists called attention to the brutal plight of the slaves and rallied support against slavery. Through their courageous efforts—protests, speeches, sermons, editorials, political campaigning and debate, hiding or rescuing fugitives—abolitionists paved the way for the end of slavery in the United States. Their struggle would be long and hard fought, however, and much blood would be shed along the way.

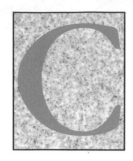

CHAPTER 2

PATHS TO FREEDOM

The Underground Railroad worked secretly and quickly. Many resourceful people on both sides of the Mason-Dixon Line had to devise strategies to free slaves, sneak them out of enemy territory (the slave states), and get them to safety. (The Mason-Dixon Line was the boundary separating Pennsylvania from Maryland—the free North from the slave South.) The agents of the Underground Railroad were waging a secret war against fugitive slave hunters. The battles were fought less with guns than with secret codes, maps, midnight journeys, disguises, and deception. Successful fugitives were always one step ahead of their captors.

"All Aboard!"

By the 1830s, trains were gaining popularity as a means of transporting goods and people. So it was only natural for the Underground Railroad to adopt the terms of this new, exciting form of American transportation to describe its operations and members.

Those who escorted slaves between safe houses—whether on foot, by boat, by horse and wagon, or even on actual locomotives—were known as conductors. The homes and businesses where fugitives hid were called stations or depots. The homeowners were known as stationmasters. Individuals who contributed money to

This photograph, entitled "Cumberland Landing, VA Group of 'Contrabands' at Foller's House," was taken on May 14, 1862, by James F. Gibson. It shows a group of about twenty escaped slaves posing in front of a cabin in Cumberland Landing, Virginia. By that time, the Civil War was raging and fugitives were beginning to flee north in record numbers.

the cause were sometimes called stockholders. Important Underground Railroad agents were often given mock titles. For example, Indiana resident Levi Coffin, who with his wife, Catharine, helped some two thousand slaves reach freedom, was sometimes referred to as the president of the Underground Railroad. As news of the railroad's expanding operations spread throughout the slave states, people began to whisper about "catching the next train" north.

Some conductors, like Harriet Tubman, an African American woman and former slave, would journey to the plantations themselves and escort the slaves personally. Other times, slaves received only an obscure message or rumor telling them where to go. All along the route, slaves would travel ten to twenty miles a night. In the South, they often had to stay in abandoned barns, caves, or other remote, secret places. Upon reaching the North, the homes and businesses of the abolitionists were their stations and depots.

Disguises

Disguises were an important tool in successful slave escapes. Blacks who had escaped earlier and returned to the South to help others flee often posed as slaves to attract less attention. A black man dressed himself in the clothes of a mourning widow, with a black veil covering his face. A young black woman could cut her hair short, put on men's clothes, and pose as a laborer. These disguises and costumes would help the fugitives pass through society without arousing much attention or curiosity.

White agents of the Underground Railroad who went to the South also found it helpful to mask their identities and activities. John Fairfield was a white conductor who employed disguises in his work to help runaways. An attractive, charismatic

One of the more astounding slave escapes was undertaken by Henry "Box" Brown. Born a slave in Virginia, Brown had a friend pack him into a box in 1849. With only a little bit of water, some crackers, and a tool with which he poked airholes into the box, Brown was shipped to Philadelphia. There, James McKim and other abolitionists opened the box and were delighted to find Brown alive.

THE RESURRECTION OF HENRY BOX BROWN AT PHILADELPHIA

man, Fairfield made himself look like the typical Southern gentleman in order to arouse less suspicion when he traveled with escaped slaves. He often used wigs and makeup to disguise himself and the fugitives in his charge. At one point, during a trip near Cincinnati, he disguised himself and twenty-eight fugitives as mourners in a funeral procession. He had even hired a hearse to complete the illusion.

Secret Messages

Since the activities of the Underground Railroad could not be spoken of or written about freely, secret codes were devised so that agents and slaves alike could communicate escape plans. For example, the word "shepherds" meant that a railroad conductor was in the area. On the way north, news that "the wind blows from the south today" warned everyone that slave hunters were nearby.

One of the more clever methods of communication involved the use of quilts. Since most slaves had been deprived of education and few could read, other means of

communication were necessary. As such, quilts were used to inform slaves about how to escape and where to go. Specific quilt patterns conveyed certain types of information. The quilts were draped out in the open for slaves to see—like wash hanging on a clothesline to dry.

Some of the images' true meanings were relatively clear. A quilted sailboat might mean that a boat was available in a nearby river. A monkey-wrench pattern might mean it was time to collect the tools needed for an escape. Other images were more obscure. A popular song in the South at that time—"Follow the Drinking Gourd"—contained information on how to escape to the free North. The gourd (a container for water) was a poetic reference to the stars of the Big Dipper, which pointed to the North Star. Thus, the drinking gourd (dipper) symbolized using the North Star, like a compass, to guide them at night to Canada. These slave quilts became a secret way of directing runaways to where they needed to go while also relaying information about possible dangers ahead.

The ways that agents and passengers of the Underground Railroad communicated with each other seemed limitless. A stationmaster in one town, for instance, told runaways that they

Quilts were used by slaves and conductors to send coded messages that would help fugitives escape along the Underground Railroad. Because quilts were commonly hung out to dry, these messages could be out in plain sight, without arousing the suspicion of plantation owners. Each quilt pattern carried a particular meaning or direction. For example, the pattern at top right is known as a wagon wheel, which signifies the wagons that were the main form of transportation for escaped slaves. The middle pattern, known as a crossroads, may refer to Cleveland, Ohio, an important meeting place and juncture of various escape routes. The bottom pattern, a star, may refer to the North Star as a guiding light for fugitive slaves on their journey to the free North.

Above left: A photograph of the "freedom steps" on the Rankin property that carried many slaves from the riverbank up to the shelter of this important stop on the Underground Railroad. *Above right:* The house of John Rankin, a Presbyterian minister and famous abolitionist, located in Ripley, Ohio, next to the Ohio River. Harriet Beecher Stowe wrote an account of a female slave and her infant escaping across the waters of the freezing river that was based on a story Rankin told her.

would find the next town's station by looking for a candle burning in the third floor of a particular house. Or perhaps a white handkerchief would be tied to a tree at the gate of a stationmaster's property. The chimney of an Underground Railroad station might be identified by the white bricks used in its construction. In the middle of the night, conductors who worked with Levi and Catharine Coffin would gently rap a certain number of times at their door to signal that fugitives had arrived. Passwords were often used to identify those who were friendly to the cause. A special handshake between a conductor and a stationmaster would also be a signal that each could be trusted by the other.

From Station to Station

Fugitives riding the Underground Railroad traveled north slowly but surely. Most routes of the Underground Railroad, whether passing through Ohio, Indiana, Pennsylvania, or New York, led to the Great Lakes. There, fugitives could be taken by boat to Canada, the only truly safe refuge for escaped slaves in North America.

Stations were often no more than twenty miles apart. This was considered the greatest distance that fugitives could cover in a night, especially if they were on foot. Many times, the group of fugitives split up and stayed in separate shelters to make it harder for slave hunters to track them. Agents of the Underground Railroad found creative ways to stall or mislead these bounty hunters.

In Henrietta Buckmaster's *Flight to Freedom*, the author relates the case of an unidentified tavern keeper in Bloomfield, Ohio. One day a family of slaves came to his door. He fed them and let them rest before they resumed their journey. Soon after their departure, the slave hunters arrived, asking if runaways had been spotted. The tavern keeper replied that he had seen them pass by and that they were about a mile up the road. This stationmaster suggested that the men should stay the night; they could easily capture the fugitives in the morning.

Every one of the slave hunters overslept the next morning when the tavern keeper failed to wake them early. Upon rising late, the hunters were impatient to get back to the chase. But the key to the stables where their horses had been placed for the night was missing, and it took some time to find it. Then, coincidentally, the horses each had a horseshoe missing. By the time the slave hunters finally found a blacksmith to re-shoe the horses, the fugitives had placed many miles between themselves and the bounty hunters. They were well

Top: Allen Walls peers from behind a fake bookshelf that once hid slaves at his house in Lakeshore Township, Ontario, Canada. Walls's great-grandfather, John Freeman Walls, turned the house into an Underground Railroad museum in 1846, one year after he escaped from bondage in South Carolina. *Bottom:* A secret compartment that allowed fugitive slaves to hide beneath the floorboards of the Lewelling Quaker House, in Salem, Iowa. The house is now an Underground Railroad museum. The handrail was added in recent years.

on their way to the next station, safe—at least temporarily—from further harassment.

Hiding Places

In the various stations along the way, agents of the Underground Railroad found ways of making their homes and businesses effective and clever hiding places for their illegal guests. Secret compartments were built in which slaves could stay for days, weeks, even months. Fake walls were installed. Holes were dug in the shafts of wells. Churches and abandoned buildings were converted to safe places where slaves were harbored.

Tunnels and other escape routes were used to move fugitives quickly but invisibly. One well-known Ohio abolitionist, Colonel William Hubbard, had a tunnel dug from his barn to the edge of nearby Lake Erie. Boat captains would wait there to usher runaways across the lake and into Canada. In Underground Railroad mythology, this station was sometimes known as Mother Hubbard's Cupboard.

Sometimes even the peculiar way a house was built made it a surprisingly effective station. In Pennsdale, Pennsylvania, an abolitionist named Edward Morris owned the Bull's Tavern. It was also known as the House of Many Stairs because there were seven staircases in the two-story building. Secret panels at the top of each staircase hid the fugitives, who could quickly disappear behind them should slave hunters suddenly arrive at the tavern.

Like the actual railroads that were beginning to revolutionize American life and commerce, the Underground Railroad was an awe-inspiring product of energy, courage, ingenuity, creativity, finesse, and brute force. It, too, would transform the landscape of the United States, eventually making it a more fair and free country, one that more closely mirrored its stated ideals.

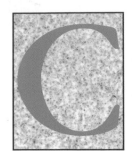

CHAPTER 3

THE FREEDOM TRAIN GAINS STEAM

Antislavery sentiment was growing throughout the United States. Many people, once cautious in their thoughts and actions, were now ready to put their own property and safety in jeopardy to hide fugitives. The risks were enormous for these people. In many states, one could go to jail for helping slaves escape. Others who were caught assisting fugitives were given heavy fines that bankrupted them. In the North, these were the risks. In the South, abolitionists were putting their lives in jeopardy. For blacks, the penalties were even harsher and often life-threatening.

Yet more and more people joined the ranks of the abolitionists every year. For them, ridding the country of the evils of slavery was worth the risk. To better understand their experiences, it is important to hear

Top: Frederick Douglass was a brilliant speaker, writer, and the leader of a new generation of abolitionists. He was arguably the most influential abolitionist because of his firsthand experience of slavery. His fight against the institution was unrelenting. Elisha Hammond painted this portrait of Douglass sometime around 1844. *Bottom:* The masthead of the June 20, 1850, issue of Douglass's abolitionist newspaper, *North Star*, which he published from 1847 to 1863 in Rochester, New York. Douglass not only fought against slavery but also for black empowerment and women's rights.

their stories. Men and women, black and white, rich and poor, these antislavery crusaders would become true American heroes pursuing the dream of freedom and equality for all.

William and Ellen Craft, Fugitive Slaves

The flight of William and Ellen Craft is an example of the kind of ingenuity and daring required of slaves to flee their masters, escape to the North, and, once safely there, preserve their new and fragile freedom. Slaves on a Georgia plantation, the Crafts devised a very risky escape plan in 1848. Since Ellen was fair-skinned, the couple decided that she would impersonate a male slave owner and that he would act as her servant.

Ellen dressed as a young Southern planter, right down to a stovepipe hat that was popular at the time. One giveaway, however, was Ellen's delicate, feminine features. To disguise them, she partially covered her face with a linen bandage to give the impression that she was suffering from a toothache. She also donned eyeglasses with dark green lenses to further mask her true identity. Since she had never been taught how to write, she put her arm in a sling so that her illiteracy could not be discovered. The plan called for William, her "trusted servant," to do most of the talking and to shield them both from discovery.

The Crafts eventually arrived in Boston, Massachusetts, after passing through Charleston, South Carolina; Baltimore, Maryland; and Philadelphia, Pennsylvania. They received a hero's welcome in the antislavery capital of New England, and people from all over the nation, even overseas, learned of their story. Having safely reached the North, however, their freedom was still not secure.

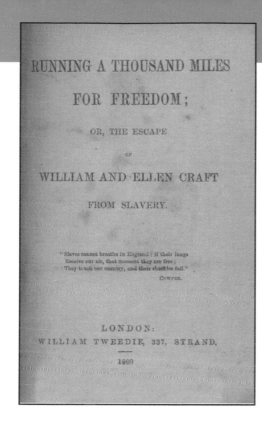

The story of Ellen Craft, pictured here disguised as a man, and her husband, William Craft, is told in *Running a Thousand Miles for Freedom*. The riveting tale of their flight from a Georgia plantation to the North and from there to England, where slavery had been abolished, was published in London in 1860. The verse on the cover page is attributed to English poet William Cowper, who wrote against slavery in the eighteenth century.

Lewis Hayden, Escaped Slave and Stationmaster

Many abolitionists were fully prepared to defend themselves and the fugitives they allowed into their homes. Among these was Lewis Hayden. Born into slavery in Kentucky in 1811, he was later sold to a Presbyterian minister. Hayden eventually decided that he could not live life as a slave. With his wife, Harriet, he fled Kentucky via the Underground Railroad. Living

Lewis Hayden, a former slave and stationmaster on the Underground Railroad, risked his life to help the antislavery cause in Boston. When the Civil War broke out, he recruited soldiers for the 54th Regiment of the Massachusetts Volunteer Infantry, the first black regiment in the North. His son perished as a sailor in the Union navy. After the war, Hayden even became a state legislator in Massachusetts, providing an inspiring example to Americans of all races of how far someone could go who was offered the freedom and opportunity to succeed. After his death, his wife, Harriet, established a scholarship for needy black students entering Harvard Medical School.

in Canada and then Detroit, Michigan, the Haydens eventually settled in Boston. There, they ran a clothing shop that doubled as a station on the Underground Railroad. They also harbored runaways in their home.

It was at this time that the Haydens crossed paths with the famous fugitives William and Ellen Craft, who had just arrived in Boston, believing they had finally gained their freedom. Yet the Crafts did not know they were being pursued by Georgia slave hunters who had arrived in town to kidnap them and return them to the South. Word spread quickly among Boston's antislavery ranks, and the city's Vigilance Committee swept into action.

The Vigilance Committees, formed in many cities where abolitionists lived, helped protect slaves who were escaping. They provided shelter, hiding places, and legal aid. At times, they even defended fugitives with deadly force.

While Ellen Craft hid in the home of respected Boston lawyer William Loring in the nearby town of Brookline, William Craft stayed at the Hayden residence in Boston. William Lloyd Garrison came to visit Hayden and Craft and found the house barricaded like a fortress. Hayden's sons were on guard, sitting around a table piled with guns. According to most accounts, Hayden himself sat in the basement with two full kegs of gunpowder. The bounty hunters eventually came to the house. Hayden and his sons greeted their unwelcome guests at the door with lit candles, threatening to set off the gunpowder and blow everyone up should the slave catchers try to set foot in their home.

To add insult to injury, the slave hunters could not find a commissioner to serve the Crafts with a warrant for their arrest. Many Boston public officials sympathized with the abolitionists. Therefore, the bounty hunters could not recapture the Crafts under Massachusetts law. The Vigilance Committee also harassed the slave catchers at their hotel and on the streets, yelling "slave hunters!" whenever they appeared. Frustrated, the Georgians eventually gave up and went home. After that, a priest legally married the Crafts, and they fled to England. Slavery had been abolished throughout the British Empire by 1834. In these unsafe times, no black man, woman, or child could be sure of his or her freedom anywhere in the United States, not even in the "free" North. The Crafts were unwilling to take any more chances and fled to a new life across the Atlantic.

Harriet Tubman, a Civil War nurse, spy, and Union scout, was most famous as an Underground Railroad conductor who helped hundreds of slaves escape to the North before the war. This photograph is believed to have been taken around 1880, long after emancipation. Tubman continued working for women's rights and took care of the old and poor up until her own death at the age of ninety in 1913.

Harriet Tubman, the Moses of Her People

Harriet Ross was born a slave, sometime around 1819 or 1820, in the slave state of Maryland. (A baby born to slaves automatically became the property of their master.) As a young child, Harriet suffered brutal whippings. When she was twelve, a white overseer clubbed her in the head after she refused to tie up a fellow slave who had tried to escape. When she was twenty-five, she married a freedman (a black man who had legally gained his freedom), John Tubman. In 1850, at the age of thirty, she made her escape.

A white neighbor sympathetic to the abolitionist cause slipped Harriet a piece of paper that told her where to find the nearest safe house. Upon reaching the station, Tubman was instructed to get into a wagon and hide under a sack. From there, she was taken north. She eventually escaped to Philadelphia, where she met William Still, the city's Underground Railroad stationmaster. Still took her under his wing, and Tubman soon joined the Underground Railroad.

Harriet Tubman would repeatedly risk her hard-won freedom by returning to the South nineteen times to lead escaped slaves north. Among these fugitives were members of her own family, including her parents. She escorted many of the former slaves to St. Catharines in what was then called Upper Canada (now the province of Ontario). She is reported to have rescued more than three hundred fugitives in her work with the Underground Railroad.

Tireless, determined, and courageous, Tubman became known as the "Moses of her people," a comparison to the Jewish biblical hero who led his people out of slavery in Egypt. She was strong and had incredible physical endurance. Many witnesses said she did not fear death at all and believed that God was watching over her. She carried a pistol for self-defense. She even carried small amounts of opium with her to help crying babies sleep so they would not endanger the mission. It is even said that Tubman considered shooting Underground Railroad "passengers" who expressed doubt and fear, wanting to turn back and return to the plantation. "You'll be free or die!" she was rumored to say to them.

Like Moses, Tubman believed it was her divine mission to free her people. She was incredibly fortunate and kept her wits about her at all times. By the mid-1850s, there was a $40,000 reward for her capture, a fortune at the time. When asked why she risked her life again and again, she would reply, "I can't die but once."

Levi Coffin, the President of the Underground Railroad

Levi Coffin saw his first slave on a North Carolina road when he was seven. A group of slaves passed by, chained and handcuffed in a line, as Levi stood near his father, who was chopping wood. He asked one of the men why they were chained. According to *Reminiscences of Levi Coffin* (1880), the man answered, "They have taken us away from our wives and children, and they chain us lest we should make our escape and go back to them." This incident opened the young boy's eyes to the evils of slavery, and from that moment he strongly opposed it.

Born in 1798 in New Garden, North Carolina, Levi Coffin was a Quaker who became involved with the Underground Railroad and helped slaves escape to freedom. In 1826, Coffin and his wife, Catharine, moved with their children to Newport, Indiana. There they ran a general store. For the next twenty years, the

Levi Coffin *(inset)*, often referred to as the President of the Underground Railroad, helped more than 2,000 slaves escape to Canada. He and his wife, Catharine, turned their home in Newport, Indiana, into one of the Railroad's most famous and busiest station stops. After staying in Coffin's house for up to several weeks, the escaped slaves would travel in the wagon pictured above, hidden in a compartment covered by bags of grain. After moving to Cincinnati, the Coffins helped another 1,300 slaves escape to freedom.

couple helped more than two thousand fugitives pass through the area on their way to the next stop on the Underground Railroad. The town became a central point in the Underground Railroad, with routes converging there from Madison and Jeffersonville, Indiana; and Cincinnati, Ohio. Not one of the escaped slaves they aided was ever recaptured. For his tireless efforts and his placement at an important crossroads, Levi Coffin became known as the president of the Underground Railroad, even though there was no such official position.

After moving to Cincinnati, Ohio, the Coffins continued their work helping escaped slaves to freedom. Their house in Cincinnati was large and could accommodate many fugitives. Some would hide upstairs for weeks without the knowledge of visitors or people who rented rooms there. Catharine Coffin often secretly took food in baskets that were hidden under fresh linens up to the slaves.

When the time seemed right, the Coffins hired horse teams to carry fugitives to the next station farther north, often thirty or so miles away. After dropping off their passengers in the next town, they would arrange for other Underground Railroad agents there to repeat the process.

Thomas Garrett

Another Quaker who fought against slavery was Thomas Garrett. Born a farmer's son in 1789, Garrett was an iron trader who settled in Wilmington, Delaware, a slave state. After joining the Pennsylvania Abolition Society, his home soon became known as the last stop on the Underground Railroad before the free state of Pennsylvania. It is estimated that more than two thousand runaways took shelter with Garrett during their flight north. Maryland authorities issued a warrant for his arrest that offered a $10,000 reward.

In 1848, the law finally caught up with Garrett. A federal court charged him with aiding fugitives. Not only did Garrett refuse to deny the charge, he also declared that he would continue to help slaves escape to freedom. The court found him guilty and issued a fine that bankrupted him. Garrett's antislavery friends came to the rescue, however. With their financial help, he was able to restart his business.

Like Garrett himself, the Underground Railroad, the agents who ran it, and the fugitives who rode it were all characterized by relentless determination, grit, and enormous strength. Though many attempts were made to halt its activities, the train just kept on rolling until all its passengers reached their destination—freedom.

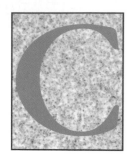

CHAPTER 4

A GATHERING STORM

As time passed, the struggle against slavery became increasingly violent. The stakes were enormous, causing emotions to run high on both sides. Abolitionists believed the nation's moral and spiritual integrity was in jeopardy, while proslavery forces felt they were fighting for their economic and cultural survival. In 1820, the North and South had hoped to strike a balance acceptable to both sides with the passage of the Missouri Compromise. The legislation deemed that all new states entering the Union would enter in pairs. A slave state could not be admitted without a free state also being admitted and vice versa. In addition, slavery would not be permitted in any new U.S. territories north of the latitude 36°30'. As an attempt to create peace between pro- and antislavery forces, the Missouri Compromise failed. Rather than creating two separate but united groups of states—one slave, one free—the ongoing acceptance of slavery that the Missouri

This is a congressional conference committee report on the bill that would become known as the Missouri Compromise. In it, the joint House and Senate committee recommends the inclusion in the bill of a provision that forbids the institution of slavery in the Louisiana Territory north of the latitude 36°30'. At the same time, it gives slave owners the right to catch escaped slaves in any state of the union. See partial transcript and contemporary translation on pages 55–56.

The committee of conference of the Senate and of the House of Representatives on the subject of the disagreeing votes of the Two Houses, upon the Bill entitled an "Act for the admission of the State of Maine into the Union"

Report the following Resolution.

Resolved.

1st That they recommend to the Senate to recede from their amendments to the said Bill

2d That they recommend to the two Houses to agree to strike out of the fourth section of the Bill from the House of Representatives now pending in the Senate, entitled an "Act to authorize the people of the Missouri Territory to form a Constitution and State Government and for the admission of such State into the Union upon an equal footing with the original States" The following proviso in the following words — and shall ordain and establish, That there shall be neither Slavery nor involuntary Servitude otherwise than in the

crimes whereof the party [ ] duly convicted; provided [ ] person escaping into the [ ] labour or service [ ] in any other State [ ] be lawfully reclaimed [ ] person claiming her or her labour or service, as aforesaid: Provided nevertheless, That the said Provision shall not be construed to alter the condition or civil rights of any person now held to service or labor in the said Territory"

And that the following provision be added to the Bill —

And be it further enacted, That in all that Territory ceded by France to the United States under the name of Louisiana, which lies north of thirty six degrees and thirty minutes North latitude, not included within the limits of the State contemplated by this act, Slavery and involuntary Servitude otherwise than in the punishment of crimes whereof the party shall have been duly convicted, shall be and is hereby

Compromise represented resulted in a wave of violence and bloodshed instead.

Open Rebellion

Even as the Missouri Compromise was passed into law, trouble was brewing in the South. In 1822, one of the most violent rebellions of the slavery era was being plotted in Charleston, South Carolina. Denmark Vesey, a charismatic and literate freeman, was planning a slave uprising. Vesey had smuggled antislavery literature into the area and often quoted the Bible when speaking against slavery.

Secretly planning the revolt in a farmhouse on an island off of Charleston, Vesey recruited followers that numbered in the thousands. They made their own weapons, including bayonets and daggers. Their plan was to burn down Charleston, then the sixth largest city in the United States, and start a revolution against slavery. An informant betrayed their plans, however, before the operation could begin. Eventually, 130 of the conspirators were arrested. Twenty-two slaves were hanged along with Vesey.

Though the planned rebellion was quashed, more and more slaves were learning about the Underground Railroad and the possible trip north to freedom. Word was spreading of new escapes all the time. It was becoming clear that the power of the slave owners was not absolute. The stage was set for further challenges to the masters and their social order.

By 1831, the activities of the abolitionists and the stationmasters and conductors of the Underground Railroad were making proslavery landowners increasingly nervous. Conspiracy theories and rumors of uprisings circulated widely. In 1831, in the middle of an economic depression, Virginia asked for more federal troops to help keep the peace, just in case.

This is the title page of *The Confessions of Nat Turner*, published by Thomas Gray, a southern physician, in 1832 in Richmond, Virginia. In this volume, the imprisoned Turner, leader of the bloodiest slave revolt in American history, tells Gray the story of the Southampton, Virginia, revolt, the reasons behind it, his escape into the woods, and the time he spent as a fugitive before his capture. At his trial, when asked if he wished to deliver any statement to the court, Turner only cited this confession. He was hanged for his crimes soon after being found guilty.

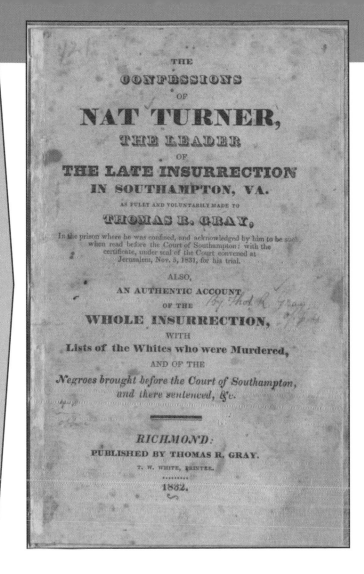

THE

CONFESSIONS

OF

NAT TURNER,

THE LEADER

OF

THE LATE INSURRECTION

IN SOUTHAMPTON, VA.

AS FULLY AND VOLUNTARILY MADE TO

THOMAS R. GRAY,

In the prison where he was confined, and acknowledged by him to be such,
when read before the Court of Southampton: with the
certificate, under seal of the Court convened at
Jerusalem, Nov. 5, 1831, for his trial.

ALSO,

AN AUTHENTIC ACCOUNT

OF THE

WHOLE INSURRECTION,

WITH

Lists of the Whites who were Murdered,

AND OF THE

*Negroes brought before the Court of Southampton,
and there sentenced, &c.*

RICHMOND:

PUBLISHED BY THOMAS R. GRAY.

T. W. WHITE, PRINTER.

1832.

The Nat Turner Revolt

That same year, Nat Turner would succeed where Denmark Vesey had failed.

Turner was a deeply religious slave from Southampton County, Virginia. He had taught himself to read and write and had recently come across an issue of the *Liberator*. He told the other slaves that he had visions of black and white angels fighting in heaven. In August, he believed he had received a sign from God that the time was right to shed blood for freedom. He gathered seventy of his fellow men with him, stole guns, and went on a rampage.

During the next twenty-four hours, they massacred every white person they encountered, going from plantation to plantation in the surrounding area. Everywhere they marched, new recruits joined them. For many hours, they met no resistance, until armed patrols finally arrived. By then, the group had killed at least fifty-five men, women, and children. They scattered into the woods, and Nat Turner went into hiding. After many weeks, Turner was found, tried for his crimes, and executed.

The Nat Turner rebellion was the single most powerful, violent revolt against slavery the country had ever seen. Blaming Turner's rebellious nature on his literacy, stricter laws were enacted to bar slaves from access to education. Any signs of disobedience were more harshly punished than ever before. The South began to look more and more like an armed camp, as militias were ordered to patrol plantation areas more frequently to prevent another such incident from happening.

Mob Violence

During the antislavery struggle, blacks were by no means the only ones to suffer from proslavery retaliation. In the North, merchants and laborers who depended on trade from the South were fiercely opposed to any change to the institution of slavery. Slavery paid the bills both south and north of the Mason-Dixon Line. When these businessmen and workers felt their livelihood was being threatened, they often reacted with violence.

In 1833, a group of activists attended a meeting of the New York Antislavery Society. A proslavery mob heard about the gathering and surrounded the meeting hall. The abolitionists had to sneak out the back door and down an alley to safety. William Lloyd Garrison, arriving the same night by ship from England, had to be secretly escorted away from the docks to protect his safety. Mob violence continued throughout that year and the next.

Many Americans sided with the abolitionists once they saw how far proslavery mobs were willing to go to preserve the institution and silence disagreement. Here, part of a poster entitled "New Method of Assorting the Mail" depicts a raid on the post office in Charleston, South Carolina, during which abolitionist literature was burned by angry mobs in July 1835. Such lawlessness and violation of the principles of free speech angered many moderate Americans and caused them to sympathize with the abolitionists.

These attacks, designed to intimidate the antislavery forces, instead began to convince many people who had been neutral in their views on slavery to embrace the abolitionist cause. In their eyes, the abolitionists were being assaulted for merely speaking their minds, for exercising their most basic rights as Americans. At the same time, the effort to halt the spread of antislavery sentiment resulted in many laws that Americans found to be oppressive. These included laws that prohibited the distribution of antislavery literature, which people felt was a violation of free speech. Some efforts to curb antislavery debate had less to do with law and more to do with lawlessness. In 1835, a Charleston, South Carolina, post office was attacked and abolitionist newspapers were burned. The 1837 murder of abolitionist publisher Elijah Lovejoy in Illinois further contributed to the impression that proslavery forces were at best opposed to basic democratic principles, such as free speech. At worst, they were cold-blooded murderers.

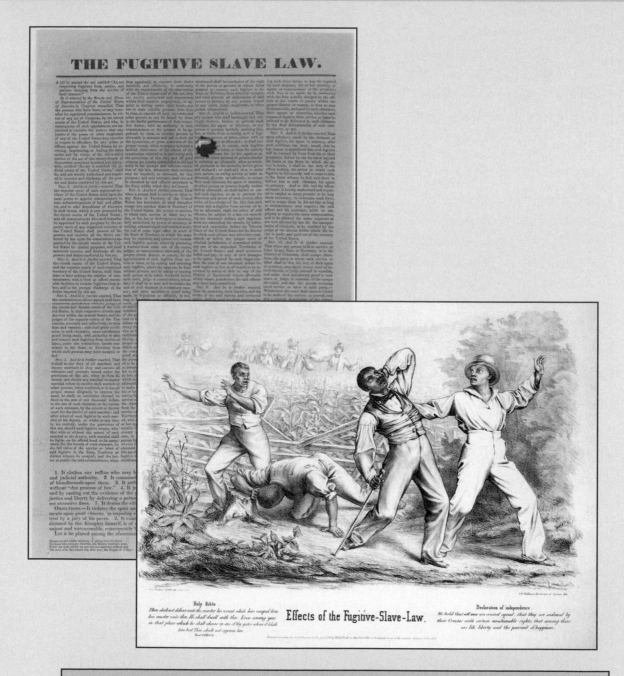

The text of the Fugitive Slave Law *(top left)* is shown here in a broadside that was printed in Hartford, Connecticut, in 1850. "Effects of the Fugitive Slave Law," drawn in 1850 by artist Theodore Kaufman, vividly depicts how harsh the results of the new measure were to escaped slaves, a group of whom are shown being wounded by the gunfire of slave catchers. Quotes from the Bible and the Declaration of Independence flank the bottom of each side of the poster to appeal to the religious and patriotic inclinations of Americans. See partial transcript of the law and contemporary translation on page 56.

The Fugitive Slave Law of 1850

In 1850, the U.S. Congress passed the controversial Fugitive Slave Law, an update of a similar bill passed in 1793. Southerners had argued that the loss of property through slave escapes to the North resulted in tremendous economic hardship. To stem their losses, slave owners would now have a law that made it easier to recapture their escaped slaves.

With the enactment of the Fugitive Slave Law of 1850, runaway slaves and free blacks were in greater danger than ever before. Fugitives could now simply be identified by an affidavit (sworn statement) of a slave hunter and forcibly taken south without any further proof or legal process. Runaways were not allowed trial by jury and could not speak in their own defense. Federal agents were now barred from preventing the capture of fugitives. It became a crime to hinder the capture of a slave in any way. Also, local police and other authorities were now required to help slave hunters in their work. The penalties for helping fugitives became harsher, with higher fines and more jail time.

Yet it was not only the roughly fifty thousand fugitives living in the North at the time who were in danger. Free blacks suddenly found themselves in jeopardy as well. Nothing could now prevent a slave hunter from kidnapping free men and women and, without any proof whatsoever, claiming them as fugitives.

The passage of the Fugitive Slave Law, far from restoring order as its supporters hoped, instead only stoked the fire of the abolitionists' anger, resulting in a new wave of violent rebellions and uprisings.

John Brown

Perhaps one of the most militant and dedicated abolitionists was John Brown. Many of his enemies, and even some allies in the antislavery ranks, thought he was a dangerous fanatic. But Brown would become one of the most powerful martyrs for the cause of abolition.

Born in Torrington, Connecticut, and raised in Ohio, John Brown pursued many professions in his life and moved around quite a bit. But wherever he traveled, whatever job he took, Brown remained passionate about one thing: ending slavery. As a child, he had seen a young black slave, a boy of twelve, beaten with a shovel. This horrifying sight, along with his father's extreme hatred of slavery, paved the way for his life's work.

Brown became very active in the Underground Railroad. One of his many business ventures was a tannery (a place in which animal skins are darkened), which he also used as a station of the Underground Railroad. He would hide fugitives in a secret basement that could be reached only through a hidden trap door. Brown also served as a conductor on the Underground Railroad and would often escort fugitives from station to station. In these efforts, Brown often worked closely with Harriet Tubman.

Bleeding Kansas

In 1854, Congress passed the Kansas-Nebraska Act. It was a direct repeal of the Missouri Compromise. Under the Missouri Compromise, the number of slave states and free states was balanced. A slave territory could not enter the Union unless a free state also entered at the same time. Now, with the passage of the Kansas-Nebraska Act, Congress left it to the voters in the Kansas and Nebraska Territories to decide whether they would enter the

Union as free or slave states. The situation quickly turned violent. Anti- and proslavery forces flocked to Kansas in an attempt to swing the vote their way. Slave owners and proslavery forces organized militias, and some tried to intimidate and influence voters at gunpoint. This threat of violence triggered what became known as Bleeding Kansas.

John Brown's five sons had already settled in Osawatomie, Kansas, and when the conflict was close to boiling over, their father followed them to the territory in 1855. By this time, Brown believed that God had chosen him to lead the fight against slavery. He fully expected it to be a fight to the death.

During the height of tensions in the following spring of 1856, proslavery forces burned the antislavery town of Lawrence, Kansas, to the ground. With four of his sons and two other followers, John Brown took his revenge. On the night of May 24, 1856, they reportedly dragged five unarmed proslavery settlers out of their beds near Osawatomie and hacked them to death with swords. (After two disputed votes that granted victory to the proslavery forces but were not officially recognized by Congress, Kansas was finally admitted into the Union as a free state on January 29, 1861, just before the outbreak of the Civil War.)

Following the violence of the election campaigns in Kansas, Brown went on to plan and lead one of the most famous escapes of the Underground Railroad. In December 1858, a slave came to Brown and asked that he help him, his wife, and his children escape before being sold by their master and separated forever. Brown soon organized an expedition that marched on two estates and liberated the man, his family, and several other slaves. From there, Brown and his men took the fugitives north to Canada on a three-week journey.

ADDRESS OF JOHN BROWN

To the Virginia Court, when about to receive the

SENTENCE OF DEATH,

For his heroic attempt at Harper's Ferry, to

Give deliverance to the captives, and to let the oppressed go free.

[Mr. Brown, upon inquiry whether he had anything to say why sentence should not be pronounced upon him, in a clear, distinct voice, replied :]

I have, may it please the Court, a few words to say.

In the first place, I deny every thing but what I have already admitted, of a design on my part to *free Slaves*. I intended, certainly, to have made a clean thing of that matter, as I did last winter, when I went into Missouri, and there took Slaves, without the snapping of a gun on either side, moving them through the country, and finally leaving them in Canada. I desired to have done the same thing again, on a much larger scale. *That was all I intended.* I never did intend murder, or treason, or the destruction of property, or to excite or incite Slaves to rebellion, or to make insurrection.

I have another objection, and that is, that it is *unjust* that I should suffer such a penalty. Had I interfered in the manner, and which I admit has been fairly proved,—for I admire the truthfulness and candor of the greater portion of the witnesses who have testified in this case,—had I so interfered in behalf of the Rich, the Powerful, the Intelligent, the so-called Great, or in behalf of any of their friends, either father, mother, brother, sister, wife, or children, or any of *that class,* and suffered and sacrificed what I have in this interference, *it would have been all right.* Every man in this Court would have deemed it an act worthy a reward, rather than a punishment.

This Court acknowledges too, as I suppose, the validity of the LAW OF GOD. I saw a book kissed, which I suppose to be the BIBLE, or at least the NEW TESTAMENT, which teaches me that, "All things whatsoever I would that men should do to me, I should do even so to them." It teaches me further, to "Remember them that are in bonds, as bound with them." I endeavored to act up to that instruction.

I say I am yet too young to understand that GOD is any *respecter of persons.* I believe that to have interfered as I have done, as I have always freely admitted I have done, in behalf of his *despised poor,* I have done no wrong, but RIGHT.

Now, if it is deemed necessary that I should forfeit my life, for the furtherance of the ends of justice, and MINGLE MY BLOOD FURTHER WITH THE BLOOD OF MY CHILDREN, and with the blood of milli... this Slave country, whose rights are d... by wicked, cruel, and unjust enactm... LET IT BE DONE.

Let me say one word furthe... satisfied with the treatment I h... trial. Considering all the cir... more generous than I expec... sciousness of guilt. I have s... was my *intention,* and what... design against the liberty... position to commit treaso... or make any general in... aged any man to do so,... idea of that kind.

Let me say somet... statements made by so... nected with me. I hea... some of them, that I ha... but the contrary is true... them, but as regarding th... joined me of his own ac... at their own expense. A... saw and never had a word... the day they came to me, an... pose I have stated. Now I h...

John B...

Printed by C. C. Mead, 91 Washington Street, and for sale at the LIBERATOR Office, 21 Cornhill, Boston.

The Address of John Brown *(above left)* is the statement delivered by the militant abolitionist *(inset)* to the court after receiving a death sentence for the events surrounding his raid of Harper's Ferry, Virginia. Upon being asked by the Virginia court if he had anything to say that might argue against a death sentence, Brown was said to have delivered the statement in a "clear distinct voice." See partial transcription on page 56.

John Brown's Raid

In 1859, Brown would meet his destiny. He had long planned to organize an armed revolt among slaves, starting in Virginia. He hoped this would spark similar rebellions throughout the slave states leading to a full-scale revolution in the South. In the summer of that year, he moved his followers to Virginia and made his move on October 16, 1859. With twenty-one men, including five blacks and four of his sons, Brown attacked and captured the U.S. armory and arsenal in the town of Harper's Ferry. Virginia militia and U.S. Marines (under the command of Robert E. Lee, who would later lead Confederate troops during the Civil War) surrounded Brown and stormed the building on October 18. Ten of Brown's men were killed in the fighting, and seven, including Brown, were captured. John Brown was eventually found guilty of treason and hanged.

Brown became a powerful symbol of a nation coming apart at the seams. His violent death made antislavery radicals more impatient to rid the United States of slavery by any means necessary. And Brown's fiery life deeply frightened the proslavery forces who now saw what lengths men would take to abolish the "peculiar institution," as slavery was called. Brown's prophetic words before his execution would come true less than a year later, with the beginning of the Civil War. According to PBS Online, Brown declared, "I, John Brown, now am quite certain that the crimes of this guilty land will never be washed away except with blood." People on both sides of the slavery issue saw Harper's Ferry as a troubling sign of things to come. A nation watched and waited for the impending storm.

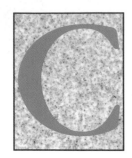

CHAPTER 5

FREE AT LAST!

Abraham Lincoln, a member of the Republican Party, was elected president on November 6, 1860. In the unstable months ahead, the Union crumbled. South Carolina seceded from the Union on December 20, 1860, followed soon by Mississippi. By early February, Alabama, Florida, Georgia, Louisiana, and Texas had joined them. On April 12, 1861, troops loyal to the South fired on Fort Sumter, a military outpost off the coast of Charleston, South Carolina. The Civil War had officially begun. Within a few weeks, Arkansas, North Carolina, Tennessee, and Virginia also seceded, and the rebellious group of states named itself the Confederate States of America, with Jefferson Davis, a Southern politician, as its president.

By late 1861, slaves were fleeing the South in droves. Shockingly, many of these fugitives, when they had broken through the Union lines, were still unsafe. Many Union officers allowed slave hunters to take these fugitives back. The Underground Railroad was needed more than ever in wartime.

Lincoln's Emancipation Proclamation of 1863 declared that all slaves living in the Confederate states were free. *Inset*: In 1892, the painter Franklin Courter was commissioned by Frances Titus, a friend of Sojourner Truth, to commemorate Truth's meeting with President Abraham Lincoln, which took place at the White House on October 29, 1864. See partial transcription and contemporary translation on page 57.

By the President of the United States of America:

A Proclamation.

Whereas, on the twenty-second day of September, in the year of our Lord one thousand eight hundred and sixty-two, a proclamation was issued by the President of the United States, containing, among other things, the following, to wit:

"That on the first day of January, in the "year of our Lord one thousand eight hundred "and sixty-three, all persons held as slaves within "any State or designated part of a State, the people "whereof shall then be in rebellion against the "United States, shall be then, thenceforward, and "forever free; and the Executive Government of the "United States, including the military and naval "authority thereof, will recognize and maintain "the freedom of such persons, and will do no act "or acts to repress such persons, or any of them, "in any efforts they may make for their actual "freedom.

"That the Executive will, on the first day

Above Ground

The Underground Railroad went "above ground" for the first time once the stream of fugitives from the South swelled into the thousands during the war. What was once an escape route for a trickle of escaped slaves suddenly mushroomed into a refugee crisis. The agents of the Underground Railroad concentrated on the areas most heavily traveled by the refugees who were escaping. Camps were set up, and volunteers helped feed and shelter the fugitives. Many volunteers also tended to those who had been wounded while escaping war-torn areas.

Harriet Tubman continued to be one of the greatest heroes of this troubled era. She nursed and cooked for Union soldiers. She also aided blacks who were sick and hungry and had escaped into Union territory. Tubman even acted as a scout and spy for the Union army, leading raids into the Confederate territories that she knew intimately.

Levi Coffin also worked hard for the new refugees fleeing slavery and war in the South. He was a leading member of the Western Freedmen's Aid Society after the Civil War. The society helped newly freed slaves by educating them and teaching them how to earn a living, as well as assisting them in securing homes, food, and clothing when needed. Coffin traveled to England and other European countries and helped raise more than $100,000 for the society. He realized that one of the most important goals of the antislavery movement should be to work against the poverty and illiteracy that were the legacy of almost 250 years of slavery in America.

Other abolitionists and Underground Railroad agents contributed in any way they could. Sojourner Truth, a black woman, collected supplies for black regiments once they were allowed

Taken by an unknown photographer, this image shows fugitive African Americans fording the Rappahannock River in Virginia in August 1862. Fleeing both slavery and the horrors of war, these refugees still had a long and hard road to freedom ahead of them. Many had been injured in war or during their escapes and had no idea what the future would hold for them. When the war started, many workers of the Underground Railroad found their efforts shifting away from sneaking a handful of escaped slaves north to trying to care for a sudden and conspicuous flood of refugees.

to fight in the Union army. After the Civil War, she even spoke on behalf of black Civil War veterans and helped them claim the land they had been promised by the Union for their participation in the conflict.

Free at Last!

When the Union army won the battle of Antietam, the bloodiest battle of the Civil War, in Maryland, in September 1862, Lincoln used the victory to move forcefully in the direction of freedom.

On January 1, 1863, he issued the Emancipation Proclamation. It declared that all slaves within the Confederacy were now free. Though the Union could not really enforce this proclamation while the war continued to be waged, it was still a powerful symbolic move. Many could now see that the end of slavery was in sight and would be guaranteed with a Union victory over the Confederacy.

By the end of 1864, the South had run out of money and the will to fight. Its armies were retreating. On April 9, 1865, the commander of the Confederate army, General Robert E. Lee, surrendered to General Ulysses S. Grant of the Union army at Appomattox, Virginia, ending the war between the states.

By December 1865, Congress had ratified the Lincoln-supported Thirteenth Amendment to the U.S. Constitution, which outlawed slavery throughout the entire nation. The Fourteenth Amendment that followed in 1868 granted citizenship to all former slaves. The seemingly unreachable goal of freedom for all slaves had finally been achieved. The abolitionists' victory took a long time but was stunning nevertheless. With the invaluable help of the Underground Railroad, slavery had become a shameful thing of the past in America.

The devastating effects of slavery continue to haunt the United States, and the road to true and complete equality remains a long and challenging one. Yet the nation today would be a far less fair and just place had the Underground Railroad not shown people the way to freedom.

PRIMARY SOURCE TRANSCRIPTIONS

Page 14: Front Page of the First Issue of William Lloyd Garrison's *Liberator*, January 1, 1831

Transcription (excerpt)

Assenting to the "self-evident truth" maintained in the American Declaration of Independence, "that all men are created equal, and endowed by their Creator with certain inalienable rights—among which are life, liberty, and the pursuit of happiness," I shall strenuously contend for the immediate enfranchisement of our slave population . . . I am aware that many object to the severity of my language; but is there not cause for severity? I will be as harsh as truth, and as uncompromising as justice. On this subject, I do not wish to think, or speak, or write, with moderation. No! no! Tell a man whose house is on fire, to give a moderate alarm; tell him to moderately rescue his wife from the hands of the ravisher; tell the mother to gradually extricate her babe from the fire into which it has fallen;—but urge me not to use moderation in a cause like the present. I am in earnest—I will not equivocate—I will not excuse—I will not retreat a single inch—AND I WILL BE HEARD. The apathy of the people is enough to make every statue leap from its pedestal, and to hasten the resurrection of the dead. WILLIAM LLOYD GARRISON. Boston, January 1, 1831.

Page 39: The Congressional Conference Committee Report on the Proposed Missouri Compromise of 1820

Transcription (excerpt)

The committee of conference of the Senate and of the House of Representatives on the subject of the disagreeing votes of the Two Houses, upon the Bill entitled an "Act for the admission of the State of Maine into the Union" — Report the following Resolutions:

Resolved:

1st That they recommend to the Senate to recede from their amendments to the said Bill . . .

And that the following provision be added to the Bill —

And be it further enacted, that in all that Territory ceded by France to the United States under the name of Louisiana, which lies north of thirty six degrees and thirty minutes north latitude, not included within the limits of the State contemplated by this act, Slavery and involuntary servitude otherwise than in the punishment of crimes whereof the party shall have been duly convicted, shall be and is hereby forever prohibited: Provided always, That any person escaping into the same, from whom labour or service is lawfully claimed, in any state or territory of the United States, such fugitive may be lawfully reclaimed and conveyed to the person claiming his or her labour or service as aforesaid.

Contemporary English Translation

The conference committee of the Senate and House of Representatives has considered the disagreements between the two Houses concerning the Missouri Compromise bill. In the portion of the bill relating to the admission of Maine as a state, we have decided that the Senate should withdraw its proposed changes . . . We have also decided that the following provision concerning the Louisiana Territory should be added to the bill:

In all the territory of the Louisiana Purchase north of the latitude 36° 30' and not part of the Missouri Territory described in this act, slavery will be illegal (though people convicted of crimes will continue to be arrested and held in prison). Slaves who escape to this territory or any other state in the union, however, can be caught and returned to their masters.

Page 44: The Fugitive Slave Law of 1850 (also known as the Compromise of 1850)

Transcription (excerpt)

7. Resolved, That more effectual provision ought to be made by law, according to the requirement of the Constitution, for the restitution and delivery of persons bound to service or labor in any State, who may escape into any other State or Territory in the Union. And,

8. Resolved, That Congress has no power to promote or obstruct the trade in slaves between the slaveholding States; but that the admission or exclusion of slaves brought from one into another of them, depends exclusively upon their own particular laws.

Contemporary English Translation

7. It is decided that, as required by the Constitution, a stronger law must be passed to require the return of escaped slaves to their masters, regardless of what state they have fled from and which state or territory they have fled to.

8. It is also decided that Congress has no right to get involved in the buying and selling of slaves that occurs between the slave states. Instead, the laws of each slave state must determine whether trading in slaves with other slave states is forbidden or allowed.

Page 48: The Address of John Brown

Transcription (excerpt)

The Address of John Brown to the Virginia Court, when about to receive the sentence of death, for his heroic attempt at Harper's Ferry, to give deliverance to the captives, and to let the oppressed go free . . .

I have, may it please the Court, a few words to say. In the first place, I deny every thing but what I have already admitted, of a design on my part to free Slaves. I intended, certainly, to have made a clean thing of that matter, as I did last winter, when I went into Missouri, and there took slaves, without the snapping of a gun on either side, moving them through the country, and finally leaving them in Canada. I desired to have done the same thing again, on a much larger scale. That was all I intended. I never did intend murder, or treason, or the destruction of property, or to excite or incite Slaves to rebellion, or to make insurrection . . .

I believe that to have interfered as I have done, as I have always freely admitted I have done, in behalf of his [God's] despised poor, I have done no wrong, but RIGHT.

Now, if it is deemed necessary that I should forfeit my life, for the furtherance of the ends of justice, and MINGLE MY BLOOD FURTHER WITH THE BLOOD OF MY CHILDREN, and with the blood of millions in this Slave country, whose rights are disregarded by wicked, cruel, and unjust enactments—I say, LET IT BE DONE.

Page 51: The Emancipation Proclamation

Transcription (excerpt)

By the President of the United States of America:

A Proclamation.

Whereas, on the twenty-second day of September, in the year of our Lord one thousand eight hundred and sixty-two, a proclamation was issued by the President of the United States, containing, among other things, the following, to wit:

"That on the first day of January, in the year of our Lord one thousand eight hundred and sixty-three, all persons held as slaves within any State or designated part of a State, the people whereof shall then be in rebellion against the United States, shall be then, thenceforward, and forever free; and the Executive Government of the United States, including the military and naval authority thereof, will recognize and maintain the freedom of such persons, and will do no act or acts to repress such persons, or any of them, in any efforts they may make for their actual freedom."

Contemporary English Translation

On September 22, 1862, the president of the United States issued a proclamation that said this, among other things:

"Beginning January 1, 1863, all people being held as slaves in any of the rebelling states will be considered free, forever. The U.S. Government, including the army and navy, will recognize, enforce, and protect the freedom of these ex-slaves and will do nothing to prevent their attempts to gain their freedom."

GLOSSARY

abolitionist Someone who spoke out against or worked to end slavery.

conductor A person who escorted fugitive slaves from station to station on the Underground Railroad.

emancipation Freedom from slavery or some other controlling, restrictive influence.

martyr A person who dies for a cause.

overseer The person in charge of guarding and punishing slaves.

plantations Huge farms in the southern United States, mostly worked by slave labor before the Civil War.

secede To quit or withdraw from a group, organization, or country.

station A stop on the Underground Railroad where fugitive slaves were hidden.

stationmaster The person who sheltered fugitives at his or her stop—usually a private home or place of business—on the Underground Railroad.

Vigilance Committees Local groups in American cities and towns that aided and defended escaped slaves.

# OR MORE INFORMATION

Charles H. Wright Museum of African American History
315 East Warren Avenue
Detroit, MI 48201-1443
(313) 494-5800
Web site: http://www.maah-detroit.org

Frederick Douglass Museum and Cultural Center
25 East Main Street, Suite 500
Rochester, NY 14614-1874
(716) 546-3960
Web site: http://www.ggw.org/freenet/f/fdm

National Underground Railroad Freedom Center
312 Elm Street, Suite 1250
Cincinnati, OH 45202
(513) 412-6900
Web site: http://www.undergroundrailroad.org

Web Sites

Due to the changing nature of Internet links, the Rosen
Publishing Group, Inc., has developed an online list of Web
sites related to the subject of this book. This site is updated
regularly. Please use this link to access the list:

http://www.rosenlinks.com/psah/unra

FOR FURTHER READING

Lawing, Charlie B. *William Lloyd Garrison and the* Liberator (World Writers). Greensboro, NC: Morgan Reynolds, 1999.

Painter, Nell Irvin. *Sojourner Truth: A Life, a Symbol*. New York: W. W. Norton & Company, 1997.

Petry, Ann. *Harriet Tubman: Conductor on the Underground Railroad*. New York: Harper Trophy, 1996.

Rappaport, Doreen. *Escape from Slavery: Five Journeys to Freedom*. New York: Harper Trophy, 1999.

Schraff, Anne. *Frederick Douglass: Speaking Out Against Slavery*. New York: Enslow Publishers, 2002.

BIBLIOGRAPHY

Blockson, Charles L. "Escape from Slavery: The Underground Railroad." *National Geographic*, July 1984, pp. 3-39.

Blockson, Charles L. *Hippocrene Guide to the Underground Railroad*. New York: Hippocrene Books, 1994.

Blockson, Charles L. *The Underground Railroad: Dramatic Firsthand Accounts of Daring Escapes to Freedom*. New York: Berkley Books, 1987.

Buckmaster, Henrietta. *Flight to Freedom: The Story of the Underground Railroad*. New York: Thomas Y. Crowell Company, 1958.

Jacobs, Donald M., ed. *Courage and Conscience: Black and White Abolitionists in Boston*. Indianapolis: Indiana University Press, 1993.

"Reminiscences of Levi Coffin." University of North Carolina at Chapel Hill Libraries. 2001. Retrieved January 2003 (http://docsouth.dsi.internet2.edu/nc/coffin/coffin.html).

Tobin, Jacqueline, et al. *Hidden in Plain View: A Secret Story of Quilts and the Underground Railroad*. New York: Bantam, 2000.

The West, "Episode Four (1856-1968)." PBS Online. 2001. Retrieved January 2003 (http://www.pbs.org/weta/thewest/program/episodes/four/thisguilty.htm).

PRIMARY SOURCE IMAGE LIST

Page 9: An 1840 American Anti-Slavery Society broadside entitled *Illustrations of the American Anti-Slavery Almanac for 1840.* Courtesy of the Rare Book and Special Collections Division of the Library of Congress.

Page 11 (left): The title page of the 1852 edition of Harriet Beecher Stowe's *Uncle Tom's Cabin*, published by John Cassell in London, England.

Page 11 (right): An 1859 poster advertising Harriet Beecher Stowe's novel, *Uncle Tom's Cabin.* Courtesy of the Corbis photography and picture archive.

Page 12: An 1856 map entitled "Reynolds's Political Map of the United States, Designed to Exhibit the Comparative Area of the Free and Slave States." Courtesy of the Geography and Map Division of the Library of Congress.

Page 14: The front page of the January 1, 1831, edition of the *Liberator*, published by the abolitionist William Lloyd Garrison. Courtesy of the Rare Book and Special Collections Division of the Library of Congress.

Page 14 (inset): An engraved illustration of William Lloyd Garrison that appeared in William Still's 1879 edition of *The Underground Railroad.*

Page 17: An 1862 photograph by James F. Gibson entitled "Cumberland Landing, VA Group of 'Contrabands' at Foller's House." Courtesy of the Photographs and Prints Division of the Library of Congress.

Page 19: A political cartoon entitled "The Resurrection of Henry Box Brown at Philadelphia," dating from the mid-1800s. Courtesy of the Photographs and Prints Division of the Library of Congress.

Page 27 (top): A circa 1844 painting of Frederick Douglass by Elisha Hammond. Courtesy of the National Portrait Gallery of the Smithsonian Institution.

Page 27 (bottom): The June 20, 1850, edition of the *North Star*, an abolitionist newspaper published by Frederick Douglass. Courtesy of the Serial and Government Publications Division of the Library of Congress.

Page 29 (left): The title page of *Running a Thousand Miles for Freedom; or, the Escape of William and Ellen Craft from Slavery*, published in 1860 by William Tweedie of London, England. This copy is housed at the University of North Carolina at Chapel Hill.

Page 29 (right): The frontispiece of the 1860 edition of *Running a Thousand Miles for Freedom*, depicting a disguised Ellen Craft. It is housed at the University of North Carolina at Chapel Hill.

Page 30: A photograph of conductor Lewis Hayden, circa 1870. Photographer unknown. Courtesy of the Museum of Afro-American History, Boston.

Page 32: An undated photograph of Harriet Tubman by H. B. Lindsley. The photograph is housed in the Library of Congress.

Page 39: An 1820 congressional conference committee report on the bill that would become known as the Missouri Compromise. Courtesy of the National Archives and Records Administration.

Page 41: The title page of the 1832 edition of *The Confessions of Nat Turner*, published by Thomas R. Gray in Richmond, Virginia. Courtesy of the Library of Congress.

Page 43: An 1835 political cartoon entitled "New Method of Assorting the Mail." Artist unknown. Courtesy of the Library of Congress.

Page 44 (top left): A copy of the Fugitive Slave Law of 1850, printed by S. M. Africanus in Hartford, Connecticut, in 1850. Courtesy of the Rare Book and Special Collections Division of the Library of Congress.

Page 44 (bottom right): An 1850 lithograph by Theodor Kaufmann entitled "Effects of the Fugitive Slave Law," printed in Hartford, Connecticut. Courtesy of the Library of Congress.

Page 48: "The Address of John Brown," a poster containing the militant abolitionist's 1859 statement to the court after receiving the death penalty. Printed by C.C. Mead in Boston, Massachusetts, and sold at the *Liberator*'s Boston office. Courtesy of the Rare Book and Special Collections Division of the Library of Congress.

Page 48 (inset): An 1859 photograph of John Brown by Black and Bachelder. Courtesy of the Library of Congress.

Page 51: The Emancipation Proclamation of 1863. Courtesy of the National Archives and Records Administration.

Page 51 (inset): A painting by Franklin Courter of Sojourner Truth's meeting with President Abraham Lincoln. Courtesy of the archives of the Historical Society of Battle Creek, Michigan.

Page 53: An 1862 photograph entitled "Fugitive African Americans Ford Rappahannock." Artist unknown. Courtesy of Instructional Resources Corporation.

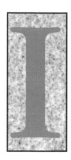

INDEX

About the Author
Philip Wolny is a writer and editor based in Astoria, Queens.

Photo Credits
Front cover, back cover (top left and bottom right), pp. 17, 19, 32, 39, 43, 44 (bottom), 48 (inset) Library of Congress Prints and Photographs Division; back cover (top right) National Park Service, artist Keith Rocco; back cover (middle left) Yale Collection of Western Americana, Beinecke Rare Book and Manuscript Library; back cover (middle right) Louisiana State Museum, gift of Dr. and Mrs. E. Ralph Lupin; back cover (bottom left) Woolaroc Museum, Bartlesville, Oklahoma; pp. 1, 9, 11 (left), 14, 41, 44 (top), 48 Library of Congress Rare Book and Special Collections Division, p. 11 (right) © Bettmann/Corbis; p. 12 Library of Congress Geography and Map Division; p. 20 (left) © Mug Shots/Corbis; p. 22 (left) The Ohio Historical Society; p. 22 (right) © Layne Kennedy/Corbis; p. 24 © AP/Wide World Photos; p. 27 (top) National Portrait Gallery/Smithsonian Institution/Art Resource, NY; p. 27 (bottom) Library of Congress Serial and Government Publications Division; p. 29 courtesy North Carolina Central University; p. 30 courtesy of the Museum of Afro-American History; p. 35 courtesy of Levi Coffin House Association and WayNet.org; p. 51 National Archives and Records Administration; p. 51 (inset) courtesy of the archives of the Historical Society of Battle Creek; p. 53 Picture Collection, The Branch Libraries, New York Public Library, Astor, Lenox and Tilden Foundations.

Designer: Nelson Sá   Layout: Les Kanturek